# RUSSIAN
## PROPLINERS &
## JETLINERS

# RUSSIAN
## PROPLINERS &
## JETLINERS

**COLIN BALLANTINE**

**Airlife**
England

# DEDICATION

This book is dedicated to my father Richard Leonard Ballantine who passed away on 21st February 1992 in Weybridge Hospital. Dad gave the best years of his life to Vickers Aircraft, Brooklands, Weybridge, Surrey.

# ACKNOWLEDGEMENTS

Over the past 30 years I have been associated with the following aviation photographers and researchers who still share my enthusiasm for Russian Airliners: Tom Singfield, Paul Huxford, Brian Stainer, Christian Volpati, Hans Oehninger, Pierre-Alain Petit, Martin Hornlimann, John Wegg. I am grateful to them and to the many friends in former Eastern Europe and the Soviet Union who put their jobs and status at risk to be involved in this fascinating hobby.

Copyright © 1993 by Colin Ballantine

First published in the UK in 1993
by Airlife Publishing Ltd.

**British Library Cataloguing in Publication Data**
A catalogue record for this book
is available from the British Library

ISBN 1 85310 381 0

Printed in Singapore by Kyodo Printing PTE Ltd.

# Airlife Publishing Ltd.

101 Longden Road, Shrewsbury SY3 9EB, England.

# INTRODUCTION

It all started when I was a teenage schoolboy in March 1956 and saw the prototype Tupolev Tu-104 land at London Airport with General Serov, head of the KGB on board. I raced home on my bicycle and told my father of my sighting . . . he suggested we both go back to London Airport, 10 miles north of our family home at Weybridge, to take a closer look. My father drove me in his 1948 Morris 10 to the central area and asked a few questions that revealed that at least another one was coming the next month. Sure enough, about 24th April 1956, three Tu-104s were parked by the side of the control tower which as most readers will know is still the original tower being used in 1992.

My father then introduced me to the fascinating world of Soviet-built transport aircraft. During the next four years sightings were few and far between. However, that situation changed when I started work and was able to commence my travels in search of these unusual aircraft, which was an adventure not for the fainthearted.

During the 1960s tension between east and west rose alarmingly and of course it became extremely difficult to gain access to the "Iron Curtain" countries especially whilst the world was witnessing the attrocities centred around Hungary, the Berlin Wall, Cuba, Czechoslovakia and Poland. At the time I tried to ignore these events and concentrate on photographing Soviet-built aircraft.

Each time I was granted a visa to visit a certain country I actually felt hatred towards the authorities knowing that

Radial piston power . . . the 1000hp Shvetsov nine cylinder engine. This reliable engine has powered over 20,000 An-2s spanning 45 years and runs like a Swiss watch.

when I arrived at their airport I would have to be subjected to questions and humiliation from immigration and customs. Once clear of the airport, the hatred became more intense when I saw normal citizens suppressed to the point that even a courteous greeting was deliberately ignored.

Behind many of the pictures featured in this pictorial is a story, too lengthy to be covered in captions. My hobby of the past thirty-two years has not been without incident, and I was often on the wrong side of the authorities.

Since 1956 about 3000 Soviet-built aircraft have passed through my camera

Below: Slov-Air utilise many An-2s for industrial work including crop spraying. OK-JIK was Polish built in 1979 and crashed beyond repair in August 1982 at Smedava whilst spraying. This colourful example is seen at Prague in the summer of 1981.

lens, some good shots, some bad shots but shooting these types of aircraft in the west is simple and safe . . . shooting them on the wrong side of the Berlin Wall was a totally different story. It then became a high risk activity and if picked up and arrested at an airport, the authorities automatically branded you as a spy. The Communist lifestyle did not lend itself to having a hobby or spare time interest. In the west you work for yourself and do whatever you wish . . . in the east you worked for the state and did as the state demanded, without question.

There are very few aviation photographers and researchers who ventured into the Iron Curtain countries prior to glasnost; this book is a pictorial record of chasing Soviet-built aircraft for the past thirty-four years, most of which have been photographed either in the Iron Curtain countries during the Cold War period or some other obscure

location under the influence of the Soviet Union. In fact with most of the world's political barriers now firmly crumbled into history, my part of the hobby has lost much of its appeal and adventure.

As far as I am concerned, it has been a terrible neglect of aviation history by the Soviet authorities in not allowing their achievements in aviation to be recorded by western historians, researchers and photographers over the past fifty years. Nevertheless, since 1987 we owe so much directly and indirectly to Mikhail Gorbachev for opening up the Soviet Union's aviation system since the inception of Perestroika.

Many years ago I set myself four goals: 1) to fly in an Il-14 — that was achieved in Poland in SP-LNG; 2) to visit Cuba — which nearly came off until a deliberate accident in Mexico City on the way to the airport aborted the visit; 3) to visit Mongolia — in fact my good friend Tom Singfield and myself used to joke about the ultimate aircraft, a Mongolian An-2, and on 2nd March 1992, the joking stopped when I shot 35 individual registered Mongolian An-2s at Ulan Bator's Buyant-Ukha Airport in sub zero Siberian temperatures; and 4) to fly around Siberia in an An-2 landing at different airstrips photographing anything in sight whether it flies or not. This ambition to cover Inner Mongolia as well as Siberia is being achieved thanks to some sincere and genuine friends in that region.

I hope the Russian authorities read this book and enjoy the pictures as much as I have enjoyed photographing them. Thank you Aeroflot and the Soviet aviation industry for making my hobby so interesting and I have even enjoyed the dangers incurred with chasing Soviet-built transport around the world.

Below: Aircraft photographs in the German Democratic Republic at the height of the Cold War period didn't come any more "high risk" than this one. It was taken in August 1972 after accepting an unofficial invitation to visit the "other side" of Berlin-Schonefeld Airport in the Interflug schitzerwagen to photograph An-2s, Il-14s, Ka-26 and Mi8 helicopters. On the day it was an adventure, twenty years later I regard it as courting a jail term! DM-WCX was one of sixteen An-2s operated by the G.S.T. Gesellschaft fur Sport and Technic, a paramilitary organisation. WCX/WCY/WCZ were Soviet-built in 1960 and withdrawn from use during 1976. Behind WCX is DM-WCZ, Interflug AN-24 DM-SBC and Air Force VIP Tu-134 177.

Below: The graphic artist at the Mlada Bolaslav Aero Club really went to town with a paint brush on OK-GIC. Pleasing to see artistic paint work on an An-2.

Right: In freezing cold Siberian temperatures Mongol-714 awaits its release from winter storage at Ulan Bator in March 1992.

Below: During a successful visit to Poland in August 1978, my taxi driver whose English was limited to "Hello, American Dollar and Good-Bye" arranged for a visit to Bemowa Airfield where Aeropol base their fleet. SP-TVN, although owned by Aeropol, was leased to the Polish Radio and Television Corporation.

Below: Originally the Hungarian Government formed four divisions of a state air operator in 1959 to perform industrial, agricultural, air ambulance and pilot training under the name of RSG-Repulogepes Szolgalat. In 1990 the RSG was restructured as Air Service Hungary encapsulating the four divisions and to celebrate the event a striking new colour scheme appeared as illustrated. HA-YHB has been on the Hungarian register since 1978, spending twelve years with the MNT as a Government runabout from Budapest-Ferihegy Airport. The Air Service fleet currently consists of sixty-six An-2s and as many Ka-26 helicopters operated from their principal base of Budapest-Budaors Airport.

Left: With the thawing of east-west relations, disarmament has taken its toll with the Soviet Air Force. The Antonov An-8s have been made redundant and handed over to Aeroflot for civil cargo use. Many Soviet Air Force An-8s were based in former East Germany at Orienanberg. CCCP-69319 had spent time with the Soviet Air Force as the patched up paintwork reveals on the tail, however, in 1978 the aircraft was a recent addition to the Aeroflot fleet and awaits its next turn of duty at Leningrad.

Below: The Antonov An-10 is basically the passenger version of the An-12 freighter of which approximately 200 aircraft were built at the Kiev factory between 1957–1960. Several accidents occurred with the An-10, most of which were caused by engine fires and structural problems from heavy landings. The last accident in May 1972 was to be the end for the An-10. All 102 passengers and six crew were killed and immediately the entire fleet was withdrawn from service. Most were subsequently scrapped and until recently only two museum exhibits were thought to exist, however, CCCP-11213 was obviously saved from the extermination campaign and resides in original condition near Leningrad.

Below: Aeroflot still operate a number of civil An-12B freighters without the rear gun turret nest. One such early example is CCCP-11129, a regular visitor to the west during the early seventies and seen here at Zurich-Kloten Airport.

Right: During November 1973 a known twenty-nine An-12s passed through Helsinki-Vantaa Airport in connection with the United Nations airlift to the Middle East. About half the Helsinki visitors were painted in air force dark grey and the remainder as illustrated were finished in Aeroflot's original red colour scheme.

Below: On its first visit to London-Heathrow Airport in 1969, LZ-BAA was operated by Bulair, a charter subsidiary of Balkan.

Right: The Soviet aviation authorities often modify a standard production aircraft for scientific research. CCCP-11530 is one such "one off" machine having been modified for Caribbean Hurricane Weather Research. The aircraft passed through Shannon Airport on its way to its new base at Havana, Cuba.

Below: First seen in 1975, Aeroflot adopted a new colour scheme of blue and white that became their standard "new look" colours. CCCP-11105 was one of the first An-12Bs to appear in the west in these colours. Seen here at Paris-Charles de Gaulle Airport operating its once weekly Moscow-Paris schedule cargo flight.

Below: Dusseldorf Airport played host to 3X-GBA of Air Guinee in July 1976. The aircraft was a rare visitor operating a flight from Conakry-Algiers-Dusseldorf. Although the aircraft is still current on the Guinee register, it has not reappeared since 1976.

Bottom: The cockpit instrument panel of LOT An-12 SP-LZB.

Below: The sole An-12 of Cubana was delivered soon after the Kennedy-Khrushchev stand-off over Soviet weaponry being delivered to Cuba. CU-T827 spent much of its time flying between Havana and Moscow carrying mainly foodstuffs to the hungry Cuban population whose international links had been severed by President Castro. The aircraft was totally destroyed when in February 1967 it exploded on approach to Mexico City Airport. At the time of the accident it was generally assumed by the world's press that the accident was the work of Cuban exiles living in Mexico City.

Below: Sigi Air Cargo is one of a number of new airlines to emerge from the political collapse of the Soviet Union and Iron Curtain countries. The attractive colour scheme has obviously enhanced the airline's potential as a commercial operator as LZ-SGA has been kept busy with commercial freight charters worldwide. Sierra Golf Alpha was previously YU-AIC operated by the Yugoslav Government and has been joined by a second An-12 from the redundant stocks of Aeroflot.

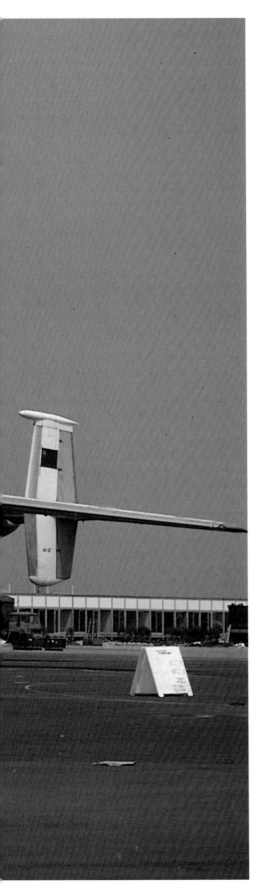

Left: Until the birth of the Boeing 747, the Antonov An-22 was the world's largest freighter. It is still the world's largest turboprop freighter with a staggering lifting capacity of 80,000 kilos in an area of 640 cubic metres. From 1971 to 1989, the An-22s were regular visitors to the Paris Air Show carrying the entire static show and a few aircraft in CKD form. This amazing looking contraprop giant is nearing the end of its days being superseded by the Il-76 and An-124 jet freighters.

Below: The business end of the mighty An-22. The navigator's position in the nose is positioned in front of the underside dome containing navigational and mapping radar. The nose radar cone contains weather and collision warning radar.

Below: Fresh from overhaul and repaint, CU-T115 of Aero Caribbean looks good in the afternoon sun during its transit stop at Prague-Ruzyne Airport.

Opposite: The Balkan Captain is taking a lot of interest in my camera as he looks up the barrel of a 200mm Nikon lens, whilst taxying out for a Sofia-Varna flight in August 1978.

Right: The Antonov An-24 has been the backbone of many airlines for 30 years. Approximately 1100 have been built and exported worldwide primarily to countries friendly towards the Soviet Union. Balkan operate thirteen examples, one of which LZ-ANC is seen arriving at the domestic ramp at Sofia in August 1978.

Below: After permission was surprisingly granted to enter the domestic ramp area at Warsaw-Okecie Airport, full advantage was taken to shoot SP-LTI. The An-24 was inbound from Krakow and is seen hurrying off the taxi-way towards the domestic ramp in August 1978.

Left: With the collapse of Eastern European Warsaw Pact forces, more Air Force transport aircraft are being made redundant and handed over to the country's civil operators. SP-LWA spent nearly twenty years with the Polish Air Force before making its entrance in full LOT Cargo Colours.

Below: Hundreds of An-26 freighters with their 5500 kg capacity are operated by foreign airlines and air forces, many of which are taken from the Aeroflot inventory. CCCP-47331 was one of six that passed through London-Gatwick on their way to Havana where they will work for the Cuban Air Force. 47331 was photographed in the early morning weak sun during December 1978. The aircraft is still current on the Cuban register as a Cubana civil freighter.

Right: Another off-shoot airline from CAAC is Air Wuhan from Hubei Province. From their base at Wuhan-Hankou Airport operate a rather nice collection of propeller driven airliners, Y-5s (An-2s), Avia 14s and Y-7s (An-24s) in a pleasant colour scheme. At most Chinese airports on the ramp an armada of bicycles peddled by ground engineers, despatchers and other airline ramp staff pounce on the arriving airliner, park their bikes against the undercarriage wheels or passenger steps until their ramp work is complete. This Chinese traffic hazard is seen as unique in the western world. As seen in the picture the despatcher being the last to leave the aircraft is peddling back to the terminal building.

Below: 5803 of the Czechoslovakian Air Force Transport Regiment is one of ten An-24s operated as VIP transports from their base at Prague-Kbely. Most of the fleet have been hidden away in Czechoslovakia for the past twenty years and seldom used.

Left: Tarom has consistently operated fourteen An-26 freighters from 1974. During 1990 five An-26s were taken over by Romavia for civilian freighting contracts. From time to time the Romanian An-26s visit Bournemouth-Hurn Airport in conjunction with the RomBac BAC-111 project.

Below: Mongolian Airlines operate four An-26 freighters based at Ulan Bator. They operate ad-hoc freight flights to Beijing and Irkutsk and rarely venture outside their region. bHMAY-3009 is being prepared for a domestic freight flight to a small airstrip in Western Mongolia.

Top right: BHMAY-6807 is one of twenty-one An-24s operated by Mongolian Airlines. Before the purchase of the Tu-154, the An-24s operated the airlines only international route Beijing-Ulan Bator-Irkutsk-Moscow. The fleet is now relegated to domestic flights covering a massive area of 1.56 million square kilometres, the majority being Gobi Desert in the south and mountain ranges in the north.

Below: Lina Congo from Brazzaville took delivery of two An-24s during 1970 for local services around the central African region. The airliners were short-lived and handed over to the Congo Air Force. TN-ABX is seen at Paris-Le Bouget after routine maintenance in 1971.

Bottom right: The An-30 is yet another ingenious design from the Antonov Design Bureau produced as a replacement for the ageing Ilyushin Il-14FG. The aircraft is ideal for countries with difficult terrain such as Russia, Mongolia, China and Bulgaria in charting vast expanses of land. Cartologists on board operate four survey cameras mounted in the cabin and aimed at the ground through underfloor hatches. The on-board computer is pre-programmed before a mapping mission to control the aircraft speed, altitude and direction. Magnetic and geophysical sensors are also carried on-board. This rare solo Mongolian example has its glass nose section covered for protection from snow and frost which is severe in a Mongolian winter.

Overleaf: This picture is not really fitting to the climate accustomed to Cubana regional airliners. CU-T880 passes through Prague-Ruzyne Airport on its long ferry flight from Kiev to Havana after overhaul and repaint. The entire Cubana An-24 fleet has been through Prague over the years for the same reason.

Below: Bulgarian Air Force An-24 030 hurries to its gate to discharge its military officers at Sofia in August 1978.

Right: The An-28, the long-awaited successor to the An-14. Little is known of its production within Russia, however, in recent years the WSK-PZL Mielec factory in Poland now produces this neat little 14-seater as a feeder liner. Approximately twenty examples have been reported with most sightings around Dushanbe in the Tadjikistan region of Russian Central Asia.

Below: Since 1988 the state airline of Nicaragua, Aeronica, has purchased two An-32s and a sole Tu-154 to supplement their DC-3, C-46 and B-707 ... what a maintenance nightmare! YN-CBV, an An-32, prepares for its long ferry flight from Prague back to the warmth of the Caribbean region.

Right: Designed as a replacement for the An-24, the general layout is similar to the BA ATP, although still retaining that distinctive Ilyushin front end. Its first appearance in the west is illustrated here at the 1991 Paris Air Show by Christian Volpati.

Right: The An-72 is a light STOL transport intended as the jet replacement for the An-26. CCCP-72000 is an early production model demonstrated at the 1984 Farnborough Air Show. At the show it was this aircraft whose pilot was warned by the authorities to tone down his enthusiastic demonstration whilst putting the An-72 through its paces. Some more recent sightings have revealed several of these aircraft painted in the Polar red colours.

Below: Mongolian Antonov tails at Ulan Bator, Mongolia.

Overleaf: One may think the An-124 is big, however, they don't come any bigger than the mighty An-225. This six-engined monster has an amazing lifting capability of 250,000 kilos in the fuselage area of 1500 cubic metres. This actual aircraft has now established the world's heaviest take-off weight at 525,000 kilos. This superb late afternoon shot was taken by my good friend Tom Singfield at the Farnborough Air Show 1990.

Right: During 1991 Heavylift joined forces with Volga Dnepr Cargo as a joint venture special projects cargo company using several An-124s. This enormous freighter is capable of carrying up to 150,000 kilos in an area of 1040 cubic metres. The An-124 has been the centre of certification problems at certain airports in the western world owing to its very heavy all up weight of 405,000 kg exceeding its nearest commercial rival, the Boeing 747 freighter.

Below: Like laying an egg in a kneeling position, the An-124 hatches out of its enormous fuselage a Kazan Helicopters Mil Mi-17. This aircraft also carried the Kamov Ka-32 helicopter and the entire Russian static display to the Avalon Air Show near Melbourne, Australia in October 1992.

Below: Commercial Ilyushins came in two piston-engined format, the Il-12 and Il-14 versions. The Il-12 was Sergei Ilyushin's first mass production design started in 1943 as a replacement for the Li-2/DC-3. These Il-12s have been extremely difficult to track down and from the latest research it appears that China is probably the only country that still has a few scattered around remote airfields. 35141 of the Chinese Air Force now resides in the Changping Aviation Museum, Changping County about 60km north-west of Beijing. Prior to its move to Changping, it was stored at Yichang then moved to Shahe by road which is about 10km from Changping. A museum well worth a visit with over 200 exhibits.

Top right: Probably the smartest colour scheme yet seen on a vintage Il-14. China General Aviation Corporation, formerly the Industrial Aviation Services Division of CAAC operate seven of these magnificent airliners and an interesting range of fixed wing aircraft fitted out as photo surveyors. Russian, American, French and German helicopters are also on hand for industrial lifting. The heavyweight department is held together with An-12s and L-100 Hercules, making China General an interesting company.

Bottom right: The 1966 Soccer World Cup produced many interesting charter flights into London. The Hungarian team and officials arrived in this beautiful looking Il-14 at London-Gatwick. The Hungarian supporters arrived the following day in a newly delivered Il-18. HA-MAE was withdrawn from Malev use in May 1970 and sold to Russia.

Below: Twenty-one IL-14s were delivered to Tarom between 1956–1960 initially for European services until the IL-18s were delivered. The reliable Il-14s were relegated to domestic routes and by 1975 most were transferred to the Romanian Air Force for a short while. Eventually they were broken up or sold to the Soviet Union along with four others. YR-ILK is seen coming off the taxi-way at Berlin-Schonefeld Airport in August 1970.

Right: This rare example of a Mongolian Il-14 has been resident in an area at the west end of the domestic terminal at Ulan Bator Airport for at least fifteen years. Unfortunately the aircraft is in fairly bad shape and is displayed rather than preserved.

Opposite: Photographing off the viewing terrace at Sofia Airport in 1978 was a risky business. Late on Friday afternoon Il-14 95 of the Bulgarian Air Force arrives with a group of military officials.

Below: When LOT retired their Il-14 fleet around 1971, one assumed the fleet would be scrapped or returned to Russia. It was therefore a surprise when in August 1978, SP-LNG together with SP-LNB of Aeropol were parked in pristine condition beyond the domestic terminal at Warsaw-Okecie. After negotiating access to the domestic ramp area, another surprise lay in store; an introduction to the Captain who offered (for some American Dollars) to fly me in this Calibration aircraft to Gdansk . . . didn't need asking twice!

Below: Looking resplendent on the ramp at Beijing Capital Airport, CAAC Il-18 B-220 awaits its next tour of duty. By 1992, CAAC withdrew their Il-18 fleet, the low hours aircraft being passed to China United Airlines, the passenger division of the Chinese Air Force operating out of Nan Yuan Air Base in the Beijing suburbs.

Right: CCCP-74259 feathers its outer props as it taxies to the "old" terminal building at Berlin-Schonefeld Airport in 1972. The aircraft, a 1968 model was built during the last year of Il-18 production.

Below: Shortly before being withdrawn from use, Tarom Il-14 YR-ILJ is seen parked on the ramp at Bucharest in company with several An-24s.

Below: A few minutes after this beautiful looking Il-14 illegally went through my camera, in went the sun and down came the rain. In this torrential rain storm the guard ignored the schitzerwagen in which I was travelling and again was able to return to the safety of Schonefeld's landside. The Interflug calibrator DM-SAL took up its position in 1968 and lasted until the arrival of its replacement IL-18 DDR-STP in 1983.

Right: Throughout the late seventies, Aeroflot Il-18s were regular visitors to Helsinki-Vantaa Airport. CCCP-75832 has just landed from Leningrad and with outer props feathered taxies into the gate area.

Left: Aeroflot's Il-18 fleet have always carried the standard blue colours, however, a small number of Il-18s attached to Aeroflot's Polar Division carry the red colour scheme and are rarely seen south of Moscow. The Polar Il-18s have in the past operated the long haul flight from Moscow to Cairo then south through Africa to Antananarivo then on to the Soviet Ice Stations on the Antarctic. CCCP-74267 is a long range Il-18D and a recent addition to the Polar fleet.

Below: Aeroflot Il-18D CCCP-75454, parked on the ramp at Berlin-Schonefeld after bringing Government officials to East Berlin in 1978. In 1990 this aircraft was reported as wfu at Pushkin, near Leningrad.

Below: This immaculate Il-18 of Aeroflot stands on the ramp at London-Heathrow north side, now the site of the Heathrow Hotel. CCCP-75404 was built and photographed in 1966.

Right: Back in 1970, enough courage was plucked up to venture outside the Berlin-Schonefeld Airport boundary to find a small wooded area close to the runway threshold. The picture of HA-MOH is one of many shot from this discreet location on the wrong side of the Iron Curtain during the long Cold War period. Unfortunately, this beautiful looking machine, Oscar Hotel was destroyed in a landing accident at Budapest claiming nine lives back in January 1975.

Below: United Arab Airlines during their 1960s flirtation with Russian-built airliners purchased four long range Il-18Ds. SU-AOY crashed into the Kyrenian mountains whilst approaching Nicosia and SU-APC after only a few days in service crashed on approach to Aswan. Both accidents claiming a total of 137 lives. SU-AOV and SU-AOX both survived long enough to be repainted in Egyptair colours during 1971. Retirement came in 1974 and both survivors were returned to the Soviet Union during 1975. SU-AOX is seen at London-Heathrow in 1969 during one of its rare visits.

Right: Out on the side of a taxi-way at Mexico City Airport, Cubana Il-18D CU-T899 looks a fine sight through a tele-photo lens. Unfortunately this aircraft came to grief in January 1985 when it crashed on to a highway near San Jose de Las Lajas shortly after take-off with engine problems. The aircraft was totally destroyed as were the 40 persons on-board.

Left: Probably the most well maintained Il-18s were the Interflug fleet with only one accident in 30 years of operations. Upon German unification seven of the fleet were retained. DM-STE originally delivered to the GDR in 1962, is seen here on the ramp at Berlin-Schonefeld Airport in August 1978. This aircraft was eventually withdrawn from use during 1989 and is now displayed at Borkheide.

Below: After the early 1960s Cuban crisis, Soviet Premier Khrushchev authorised substantial assistance to the west African nations of Ghana, Guinea, Mali and Mauritania. Air Mali from their base at Bamako leased four Il-18s initially in a mixture of Aeroflot colours and Mali registrations, followed by standardisation of the new Air Mali colour scheme in 1962. The Il-18 fleet operated to neighbouring African countries with a weekly inter-national service to Geneva and Paris. TZ-ABE is seen at Paris-Orly in July 1974. One month later Bravo Echo came to grief when on approach to Lingomin, Upper Volta ran out of fuel and crash landed with the loss of 47 lives including the crew.

Below: In 1975 Malev adopted a new colour scheme for its Il-18 fleet. HA-MOG is seen here at Zurich-Kloten shortly after its re-paint. After serving Malev for 24 years it was withdrawn from passenger service in 1988 and is now displayed at Sinsheim, Germany.

Opposite: Malev converted two passenger Il-18s to freighters, being HA-MOA and HA-MOE. Both aircraft lasted four years as freighters being pensioned off in 1987. Oscar Alpha served Malev for 27 years and Oscar Echo for 24 years.

Left: The calibration aircraft of Eastern Europe were elusive machines normally being parked far away from prying eyes or based at a military transport base. DDR-STP was taken from the Interflug fleet in 1983 replacing the ageing Il-14 DDR-SAL and fitted out as a full calibrator. Tango Papa is seen here at Berlin-Schonefeld Airport. Since unification the aircraft now faces a short future.

Below: With the swift and savage destruction of Interflug in 1990, the ageing Il-18s stood little chance of survival. Two recently converted Il-18 freighters were snapped up at bargain prices by Polnippon, a joint venture Poland-Japan air cargo company established in 1990. Little is known of Polnippon Cargo, however, after three years of cargo operations SP-FNB and FNC are still going strong from their base at Warsaw-Okecie.

Below: Since its inception in 1946 the Czechoslovak Government airline previously known as the LOFMV have operated a wide variety of Russian-built airliners for VIP flights, Government trade delegations, airline pilot training and occasionally substituting for a CSA schedule flight. OK-BYP was one of a pair of Il-18s that were rarely seen outside eastern Europe. Bravo Yankee Papa was a long range 35-seater VIP version that operated from new in 1962 until transferred to CSA in 1971 as OK-PAI. Its sister Il-18, OK-BYZ also went to CSA as OK-VAF and both airliners were the only two Il-18s to be painted in the red OK colour scheme. Both were retired in December 1989. Bravo Yankee Papa is seen on the Paris-Orly taxi-way in 1968 just prior to the Soviet suppression of Czechoslovakia.

Right: For admirers of large turboprop airliners, the Ilyushin Il-18 shares the same good looks as the Vanguard and Electra. A Russian employee of Aeroflot once told me that an Il-18 is like a beautiful woman from Siberia, sleek fuselage, elegantly powerful, incredibly good looking, but smokes too much! He was absolutely correct, this airliner is good looking and a pleasure to fly on. Just over 600 were built from 1957 to 1968 at Factory No. 30 Khodinka where the completed aircraft were taken by road to Moscow-Vnukovo Airport for their first flight. From 1974, many redundant Aeroflot examples were converted to freighters (same as Vanguard-Merchantman) at Factory No. 402 Moscow-Bykovo. Most Aeroflot versions have been disposed of, however in 1993, Cuba, North Korea, Romania, Bulgaria, Poland, Germany and China still operate the Il-18 in small numbers.

Below: A pair of Il-18s at Prague-Ruzyne
Airport, OK-PAE and OK-PAG. Both aircraft
were built in 1961, both were withdrawn
from CSA service in 1980 and both became
restaurants. What a lovely way to spend a
wet Sunday afternoon . . . sipping coffee in
an Il-18.

Below: LZ-BES was one of two Bulgarian registered Il-18s that never carried the familiar red Balkan colours. The aircraft, a basic model Il-18V, and manufactured in 1965 was delivered new to Tabso. Three years later it was transferred to Bulair, the newly-formed charter subsidiary of Bulgarian Air Transport. Echo Sierra crashed after take-off from Sofia outbound to Algiers in December 1971. All 30 passengers and crew were killed. The aircraft is seen moving gently down the Zurich taxi-way past the spring flowers that once bloomed freely on the grass verges of the airport in April 1969.

Below: The elusive Il-18s have always been the North Korean examples. From the late-sixties to the mid-seventies they were fairly regular visitors to Berlin-Schonefeld Airport flying in raw recruits to a Military Academy (as we know it . . . a School of Espionage). Into the 1980s the Il-18s from Pyongyang have frequented Prague more than Berlin, however, their role whether civil or military flights have been taken over by the Tu-154 and Il-62.

Right: Balkan Airlines have had a long association with the faithful Il-18 since 1961. A few of the original fleet, including LZ-BEK, have carried the colours and titles of Bulgarian Air Transport, Tabso and Bulair in blue and white, then came the Balkan and white colours with Cyrillic lettering, followed by a modified red scheme with Balkan titles in English and finally the latest paint scheme of green and red stripes. LZ-BEK is seen on short finals at Berlin-Schonefeld Airport during 1977.

Below: In the late afternoon winter sun at Stockholm, SP-LSH awaits clearance for take-off to Warsaw. Sierra Hotel was retired in April 1989 after 23 years' service with LOT. In January 1990 the airliner was purchased by a private owner... admire his choice of airliner.

Right: Close up of a LOT Il-18 tail bearing the original colours.

Left: During the height of Soviet support in Vietnam, the airline, Hang Khong Vietnam took delivery of three long-range Il-18Ds for their prestige route from Hanoi to Moscow. A fourth example was purchased from Mauritania. When the first Tu-134 jets arrived in 1977, the Il-18s were relegated to domestic and local international routes. VN-B196 built in 1967 and delivered from Aeroflot surplus stocks is seen at Bangkok-Don Maung Airport in March 1981 operating the twice weekly flight from Hanoi. Very soon after the Tu-134s took over this route and the Il-18s vanished overnight to spend their existence decaying in the killing fields of Vietnam.

Below: Polish holidaymakers normally head south to the Black Sea resorts of Varna and Bourgas. Here SP-LSH arrives at Varna with 120 sun-seeking Polish citizens during August 1978. Sierra Hotel was the last LOT Il-18 to wear the old colour scheme.

Below: 3X-GAT the latest surviving Air Guinee Il-18 parked at Geneva. This immaculate looking aircraft was retired at Conakry in 1984 and currently its fate is unknown.

Right: This later model Tarom Il-18D YR-IML proceeds up the taxi-way at Zurich-Kloten on its return flight to Bucharest on a sunny spring afternoon in 1977. This aircraft took the Romanian National Soccer team to Mexico City for the 1970 World Cup together with YR-IMK.

Below: The fourth Interflug Il-62 DM-SEF at Berlin Schonefeld. Echo Fox was delivered in 1971 and lasted eighteen years until 1989. The aircraft is now preserved at Leipzig as one of the many Interflug monuments scattered around former East Germany.

Right: Aeroflot Il-62M CCCP-86614 had a relatively short life of two years. In May 1977 it was preparing to land at Havana whilst operating SU331 Moscow-Frankfurt-Lisbon-Havana when on a night time approach flew into a row of power lines running through a palm tree plantation. The aircraft caught fire, broke up on impact and surprisingly two passengers walked away suffering from shock! Sixty-eight were killed.

Bottom: A regular visitor to the west during the early 1970s was the Yugoslav Air Force VIP Il-18 73201. Seen here on one of several visits to London.

Below: London-Heathrow occasionally plays host to some interesting VIP transports. T-001 of the Afghan Air Force is an Il-18E with a 35-seat VIP interior. Here it is being attended to on Heathrow's south side during December 1971.

Right: Occasionally JAT used YU-AIB on schedule service. Its official owner from 1967 was the Yugoslav Government until 1978 when it was sold to Air Guinee as 3X-GAX. They promptly crashed it into swamp land near Conakry. What a waste of a good Il-18. Seen here in better days at Geneva.

Below: The fourth Interflug Il-62 DM-SEF at Berlin Schonefeld. Echo Fox was delivered in 1971 and lasted eighteen years until 1989. The aircraft is now preserved at Leipzig as one of the many Interflug monuments scattered around former East Germany.

Right: Aeroflot Il-62M CCCP-86614 had a relatively short life of two years. In May 1977 it was preparing to land at Havana whilst operating SU331 Moscow-Frankfurt-Lisbon-Havana when on a night time approach flew into a row of power lines running through a palm tree plantation. The aircraft caught fire, broke up on impact and surprisingly two passengers walked away suffering from shock! Sixty-eight were killed.

Below: The power of the telephoto lens can enhance a picture such as framing the Cubana Il-62 with other aircraft. During May 1978, CU-T1208 had recently arrived from Moscow on route for Havana. In 1978 it was still a risk shooting aircraft from Berlin-Schonefeld's new terminal roof as hi-jackings to the west were still occurring from Berlin, Warsaw and Prague, hence the airport guards were somewhat suspicious and on some occasions . . . trigger happy.

Bottom: B-2020 is one of five Il-62s that operated the Beijing-Karachi-Bucharest route in conjunction with the Tarom Il-62s and is seen on its stopover at Karachi in December 1984. The CAAC Il-62s are firmly retired and laid up at Beijing Capital Airport.

Below: In January 1974 five basic model Il-62s appeared on routes to the west in a non-standard Aeroflot colour scheme that looked more appealing than the previous or current design. CCCP-86701 was one such aircraft and together with the other four was repainted to the now familiar Aeroflot colours.

Below: Aeroflot Il-62M CCCP-86622 once the pride of the international fleet, now relegated to routes within Russia. With flaps fully extended 86622 still speeds past the camera before landing at Berlin-Schonefeld in August 1978.

Top right: During the late 1970s, Mozambique accepted Soviet military aid that spilt over into the purchase of two civil passenger airliners. The Presidential Tu-134A was blown up whilst flying between Mozambique and south-east Africa in 1986 and the sole Il-62M purchased in 1984 is still current. C9-BAE like the Angolan Il-62s are rather rare visitors to the western world and difficult to photograph in their home countries.

Bottom right: Many Aeroflot Il-62s will be gradually transferred to the Commonwealth of Independent States newly formed airlines. Uzbekistan from their base at Tashkent (which is also the location for Russia's big Il-62 maintenance and rebuilding facility) operate seven ex-Aeroflot Il-62Ms all of which are low hours ex-Interflug airliners most of which were rarely used by the East German Government. 86579 was delivered new to Interflug in 1985 as DDR-SET, upon reunification it became D-AOAK then sold back to Aeroflot.

Below: For lovers of Russian-built aircraft and Interflug this is a priceless view. DM-SEC stands surrounded by Tupolev 134s and Il-18s at Berlin-Schonefeld twelve years before unification.

Below: Cubana have operated fifteen Il-62Ms since 1977 mainly on their routes from Havana-Madrid-Berlin-Moscow. Prior to their delivery to Cubana CU-T1208 and CU-T1209 spent many weeks crew training at Berlin Schonefeld. The Il-62s also operated the Havana-Mexico City route where CU-T1209 is seen turning off the taxi-way and heading towards its parking area.

Left: OK-ABD looking majestic, makes a fast final approach at Berlin-Schonefeld in July 1972. The aircraft was delivered to CSA in March 1970 and retired in September 1984 after 20,297 hours performing 7664 landings.

Below: Malev has traditionally been a user of Soviet-built short to medium range airliners and whilst the airline was creating history as the first former Iron Curtain country to operate the Boeing 737, an Il-62M slipped quietly on to the Hungarian register. HA-LIA was leased from Aeroflot in full Malev colours from June to September 1991. The airliner was returned to Russia after three months' use and is seen here awaiting patronage at Budapest-Ferihegy Airport.

Below: SP-LBG was one of LOT's Il-62Ms. Regrettably Bravo Golf crashed near the airport while trying to return to Warsaw-Okecie after two of its engines caught fire shortly after take-off. All 183 passengers were killed. This was the second misfortune with a LOT Il-62, SP-LAA had a similar fate.

Bottom: Whilst awaiting delivery of their Il-62Ms, LOT chartered CCCP-86663 to supplement their Il-62 routes. The charter lasted for the summer of 1978. Pictured at London-Heathrow in June 1978 on push-back prior to its departure back to Warsaw.

Below: Between April and November 1971, Aeroflot and KLM established a joint venture once weekly service between Amsterdam and Moscow resulting in four Il-62s wearing small KLM titles. One such example is CCCP-86652 taking off from Zurich-Kloten.

Below: Iraqi Airways is believed to be the largest user of the Il-76 outside Russia. Deliveries started back in 1979 and a known 38 examples were recorded up to the start of the Gulf War in January 1991. Many of the Il-76 fleet are painted in the airline's attractive two-tone green colour scheme with a smaller amount finished in a drab two-tone grey colour with smaller Iraqi Airways titling. Throughout the 1980s, sightings have been frequent at Paris Orly, Prague-Ruzyne and Berlin-Schonefeld Airports, all three cities being a good source of supply for aircraft spares and fighting machinery. At the time of writing it is not known how many Il-76s survived the Gulf War

Below: CAAK of North Korea is the latest operator of the versatile Il-76MD.

Bottom: 5A-DNS was originally with Jamahiriya Air Transport but now carries the more respectable titles of Libyan Arab Airlines. November Sierra was one of two Jamahiriya Air Transport Il-76s to be impounded, at Manaus, Brazil in 1983 for carrying "suspect" cargo that wasn't quite the same as the manifest stated . . .

Below: A small amount of Il-76s of Aeroflot carry this attractive red colour scheme commonly known as polar colours. Basically, an aircraft wearing red is easier to see than the normal Aeroflot blue especially in polar and Siberian regions during their harsh snowy winters. CCCP-76479 has visited Prague on a few occasions to pick up spares for the Czech-built L-410, many of which operate in the Siberian Far East.

Below: Front end of CCCP-76460. Probably the most successful, reliable and economic aircraft to come out of Russia since the post-war years. In keeping with Russian transport tradition, the Il-76's front end houses the navigator/observer position and of course is useful for instant military application.

Below: CCCP-76460 is a basic commercial Il-76T freighter operated by Aeroflot in standard colours. This aircraft together with others in the same serial range are frequent commercial cargo visitors to the west.

Bottom: Similar to Iraq, it is not really known which Il-76s are flown by either Libyan Arab Airlines or Jamahiriya Air Transport as both companies have intimate military connections. Originally five Il-76s were painted in full Libyan Arab Airlines gold and white colours and any aircraft registered 5A-Delta November was the property of Jamahiriya Air Transport and carried their titles. During the mid-1980s the twenty-three known Il-76s appeared to be operating with mix and match colours and titles. Prague and Berlin were the safest places to view these aircraft if you weren't game enough to visit Tripoli!

Top: A glimpse into the Aeroflot future. The Ilyushin Il-96 is similar in size to the Airbus A-310 and is due to enter Aeroflot service in the early 1990s. CCCP-96000 is seen at the Paris Air Show and photographed by long time friend Christian Volpati.

Bottom: The Il-86 was the former Soviet Union's answer to the western world's wide-bodied airliners first appearing back in 1976. To date Aeroflot have been the sole operator with approximately 130 examples being built. The Il-86s used for long haul domestic routes are fitted with 350 economy seats and international versions are fitted for 20 first class and 296 economy. No doubt as the airlines of the C.I.S. establish themselves the Il-86 will be seen in other colour schemes. CCCP-86104 is seen operating a series of lease flights for Greenair of Turkey during 1991. This airliner is the only Il-86 to carry non-Russian titles of Greenair.

Below: Until 1990 Balkan operated eleven Mi-8 helicopters in three versions, industrial, passenger and VIP. All were fitted with round cabin windows except the two VIP versions that were fitted with large panoramic windows complete with curtains. Nine of these Mi-8s have now passed to Heli Air Services including LZ-CAE, leaving Balkan with two examples.

Bottom: Two of three Mongolian Mil Mi-8 helicopters appear in this picture at Ulan Bator in February 1992. They are used for a variety of tasks including industrial lifting around Ulan Bator City, mineral exploration and research in the Gobi Desert and are also available at enormous expense for the rich man's sport of chasing and shooting bears and deer in the northern forests of Mongolia.

Below: OK-DXN has been with Slov-Air since 1973. One of four Mil Mi-8 helicopters used for industrial lifting and various cargo work utilising the large camshell rear doors.

Below: In an effort to reduce revenue losses from empty seats, LOT secured five Yak-40s from the Polish Air Force Transport Regiment. Smartly painted in LOT colours the Yak-40s operate short haul routes radiating from Warsaw and Gdansk carrying a maximum of 28 passengers. These Yak-40s were a stop-gap until the arrival of the ATR-72s.

Right: An Il-18 tail of three CSA Yak-40s at Prague . . .

Below: Between 1974 and 1978, CSA took delivery of seventeen Yak-40s as a domestic replacement for the Il-14s. The fleet was diminished to six aircraft and as they become due for overhaul are being repainted in the new CSA livery.

Bottom: Many of Angola's transport aircraft both civil and military have been blasted out of the sky by guerrilla rockets during the recent years of the Government's power struggles. This TAAG Yak-40 has been involved in an accident and subsequently repaired, Taking a risk is flying on an Angolan domestic flight!

Below: General Air of West Germany obtained certification to operate the Yak-40 on domestic routes, a flirtation with Russian-built airliners that ended in disaster. Bravo Bravo was delivered in June 1972 and by November of that year the five aircraft were fully operational, but not without their problems. Brave Delta overshot the runway at Saarbrucken, hit a tree and ended up in a trench. General Air ceased operations in October 1975 with the remaining Yak-40s being returned to Riga.

Right: The Yak-42 tri-jet was intended as a replacement for the Tu-134, however, after an accident at Krasnodar in 1982 the type was grounded until October 1984 for modifications before production re-started. CCCP-42544 was acting as a demonstration model at the 1985 Paris Air Show.

Below: The Soviet Union's first jet airliner, the Tu-104 entered passenger service in September 1956 and lasted until November 1979. Approximately 200 examples were built, however, the same twelve aircraft seemed to cover Aeroflot's routes to the west. CCCP-42430 was one of the rare Tu-104Bs to venture outside the Soviet Union and is seen here on a high speed approach to Berlin-Schonefeld in August 1974. The aircraft is fresh out of overhaul and the paint shop.

Left: The last CSA Tu-104 to be retired. OK-LDC prepares to take-off from Copenhagen-Kastrup in June 1972. This aircraft was eventually moved by road from Prague-Ruzyne to Touzim for display in a recreation area in the middle of a housing estate. From a fleet of six only three survived and displayed at Kbely, Touzim and Olomouc. Bravo, Delta and Echo met with accidents at Bombay, Tripoli and Nicosia respectively.

Below: The magnificent looking Tu-104 became a regular weekend visitor to London-Gatwick during the 1971–1973 package holiday season. CCCP-42439 approaches the end of Gatwick's south terminal finger on one of its many visits.

Below: It was not surprising when Aeronica of Nicaragua added a Tu-154M to its civil fleet in 1989. Since the early eighties a steady flow of Russian-built aircraft have been filtering into the FAS-Fuerza Aerea Sandinista operated in a dual civil-military role.

Right: One can wait a long time at the airports of east and west Europe for a Syrianair Tu-134. In December 1984 a visit was undertaken resulting in this mid-morning portrait of YK-AYE at Damascas. Originally delivered during 1982 for Government use, the six aircraft have gradually been transferred to Syrianair for civil schedule flights.

Top right: Since 1985, CAAC have been slowly disecting their civil aviation structure into competitive corporations with their own identity. As the CAAC Tu-154s are becoming due for overhaul they are being repainted in their new company livery, the most striking so far have been China South-west Airlines with B-2618 looking good in the Beijing sun.

Centre right: 1407 has been on the books of Czechoslovakian Air Force as a VIP transport since 1971 and has carried the civil registration of OK-AFD for Government flights of convenience. The aircraft, now over twenty years old, has spent most of its time as a seldom used VIP transport based at Prague-Kbely Airbase about 30 kilometres west of Prague.

Bottom right: The first forty-four Aeroflot Tu-154s were delivered in the pre-1975 livery similar to the early Tu-134s. Very few of these early models in the old colours were seen in the west, however, they were regulars at Berlin and Prague.

Opposite: CU-T1224 was the second Tu-154 to be purchased by Cubana in July 1981. Whilst waiting for this aircraft on short finals at Mexico City Airport in August 1982, it decided to take a short cut and dispense with the formalities of the glide path, hence the unusual angle.

Left: Loas Aviation took a very short-lived lease in the form of Balkan Tu-154 LZ-BTN whilst waiting for the delivery of the Loas Aviation Boeing 737. Bravo Tango November is seen here at Bangkok-Don Maung Airport moving on to Gate 28 on its once weekly flight from Vientianne. The colour scheme is part Balkan with Loas titles and the country's emblem on the tail. The picture was shot just prior to the lease finishing in January 1992.

Below: Tow tugs view of Loas Tu-154 on pushback at Bangkok.

Below: Aeroflot Tu-154B drifts into Frankfurt on its first visit to the west in 1977.

Bottom: Pending the delivery of their own Tu-154 tri-jet airliners, LOT leased Aeroflot Tu-154 CCCP-85455 in full Aeroflot colours with LOT titles. The aircraft in this guise was operated from June 1985 to June 1986.

Right: Aeroflot Tu-154A CCCP-85109 as seen through a short telephoto lens hurries down the taxi-way at Vienna-Schweikart Airport in May 1976.

Below: When the first LOT Tu-154 was delivered, CCCP-85455 was painted in full LOT colours for another twelve months before being returned to Aeroflot. The tail engine housing was painted blue on 85455, on the Polish registered Tu-154s the housing is white.

Bottom: Cockpit layout of a Balkan Tu-154.

Below: In 1968 Aviogenex was formed as a package holiday airline selling direct to the vast European holiday market. A few borrowed aircraft were used untl the first Tu-134 was delivered. YU-AHI as illustrated was delivered in March 1969 and returned to the Soviet Union in 1971 in exchange for the later model Tu-134A.

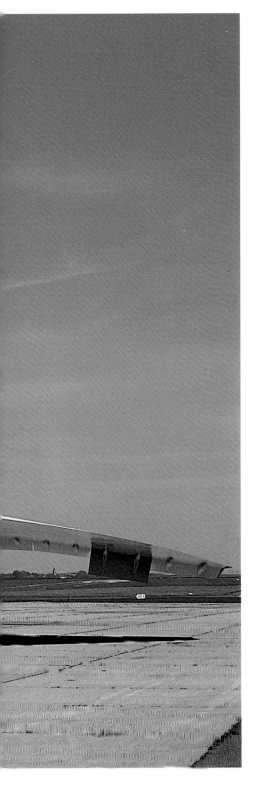

No book on Russian aircraft would be complete without shots of a Tu-144 commonly know as the Russian Concordskii. These unusual views of CCCP-77110 come of course from the Paris Air Show of 1977. This actual aircraft is now displayed at the Ulyanovsk Museum.

Below: A small amount of Aeroflot Tu-134s in a specific serial range were painted in this attractive blue colour scheme during the mid-1970s. It has never been established why or which Aeroflot directorate operated these aircraft.

Bottom: The early production Tu-134s from 1968 to 1975 carried this very basic Aeroflot colour scheme. Most of the early versions have faded into history and been scrapped. Two are known to be displayed in Russia and another is used as a cabin trainer at Leningrad.

Below: Whilst awaiting permission to gain access to the ramp area of Varna, the viewing area on the roof of the terminal building can be very interesting watching Russian-built aircraft come and go with the intense holiday traffic. OK-HFL CSA Tu-134A taxies in after its flight from Prague during August 1978.

Right: In 1976 the East German Air Force handed 177 over to Interflug as DM-SCZ. During April 1986 the aircraft was flown to Dresden, retired and displayed at Bernsdorf about 100 kilometres from the famous Colditz Castle. Charlie Zulu is approaching Berlin-Schonefeld Airport in August 1978, shot discreetly from behind my favourite cluster of bushes.

Below: The Angolan Government Tu-134A is somewhat of a rare bird. D2-ECC has made a very limited number of flights outside Angola. In November 1981 Paris played host to Echo Charlie Charlie.

Left: Twenty years ago in 1972 this Balkan Tu-134 was caught on short finals at Berlin-Schonefeld in its old red colours and Cyrillic titles. This aircraft LZ-TUC had not had its tail bullet modified and extended. In western circles the centre air brake is known as the "barn door".

Below: During July 1972 an Eastern European Heads of State conference took place in East Berlin. The various Presidents arrived in their VIP interior jet to discuss the future . . . The Bulgarian Head of State arrived in LZ-TUP painted in an unusual colour scheme. It was the only aircraft that was parked in a somewhat difficult position and a few risks had to be taken to obtain this shot, however, framed by the trees and bushes gives the picture a kind of sinister appeal.

This megalithic Tupolev Tu-114 is still credited as being the world's fastest turbo-prop airliner with a maximum speed of 870km/h or 540mph. Unfortunately very few of these beautiful giants were seen in the west during their heydays of the mid-1960s. The interiors of the Tu-114s were fitted with lavish wooden carved tables and brass lamps all fitted into a Victorian style cabin. The prototype stands in front of the Pan American terminal under construction at Idlewild International Airport in September 1959. On this occasion Prime Minister Khrushchev and other Russian officials were flown in 5611 non-stop Moscow to New York in 11 hours 5 minutes, an excellent effort for a turboprop airliner.